A Christmas Journey

...through poetry

One poem for each day of the Christmas season

By

Mitchell S Smith

Christmas Time

This collection of poems is a mix of spiritual, comical, satire and some are even full of sadness. But isn't that really what encompasses the Christmas season around this world? Christmas is not a joyful and much awaited event for some. It is a time that many wish does not come once a year... or ever. For many it brings the sadness of past events, lost loved ones and broken hearts back into focus and fresh remembrance.

I hope reading this Christmas Journey through poetry is uplifting and it warms your heart. May the spirit of Christmas return to you if it has long since departed through reading these simple poems. If you are already filled with the Christmas spirit, I pray this just enhances what you already enjoy and may it encourage you to share what Christmas is really all about with others.

Mitch

Luke 2: 10, 11

Merry Christmas!

Luke 2:10 *and the angle said unto them, fear not; for behold, I bring you good tidings of great joy, which shall be to all people. For unto you is born this day in the city of David a Savior, which is Christ the Lord.*

Poems

Unspeakable

A Season of Change

My Christmas Tree

Christmas Joy

Christmas Star

His Name

Christmas Morning

Lights

Eyes So Blue

A Christmas Scene

Kings on Bended Knee

Winter Heart

First Night

Voices Fill the Sky

I Said Goodbye

The Gift

Embers of My Dreams

Christmas Gift

God Walked In

Snowflake

Christmas' Missed

Christmas Time

Papa's Christmas

Never the Same

<u>*Unspeakable*</u>

No snow on the ground

No one jolly and round

No cookies and milk to leave

No sleigh bells ringing

No carolers singing

No reindeer on Christmas Eve

No trips to the mall

No lights to install

No parades marching downtown

No fighting the crowd

No snow to be plowed

One night, one Gift, one crown

Good news to some

The Holy One

Greatest Gift the world's ever known

Wrapped up in hay

In a humble array

A lowly manger for a throne

Unspeakable Gift born

That first Christmas morn

God's gift...beyond compare

Our God's only son

Unspeakable One

Jesus... this Christmas...to share

A Season of

Change

A look in the glass

A look deep inside

Change has visited you

A wrinkle...a frown

A heart gone cold

Change...from out of the blue

From falling leaves

To falling snow

The air now bitter cold

A joyful smile

A spirit sweet

Have gone to parts untold

Asleep...alone

In deepest night

A dream...or was it real?

Long years ago

A child was born

The Gift no one can steal

The birth...the cross

His saving grace

Lost...as memories fled

This Christmas time

The cold...the gray

Change to crimson red

Daybreak brings

A joyful heart

Thanksgiving floods within

One night a dream

At mornings light

A season of change

...can begin

My Christmas Tree

Majestic, in the moonlight
Bluish green and snowy white

Ten feet tall it stands alone
Forest deep and out of sight

The fire, it snaps and pops
Hot chocolate in our hands

Children trim the tree with
White lights and silver strands

Gold star placed on its tip
Our lanterns all turned low

We decorate my tree as
The songs play soft and slow

We're all singing silent night
Holding hands, 'round the tree

The Christmas spirits here
In our hearts, our family

I'm thinking back tonight
To those childhood memories

Season's lights...everywhere
Joyful spirit in the breeze

My friends and neighbors too
In our home Christmas Eve

I remember as my tears
Fall so gently on my sleeve

Now a man, old, alone
In my mind I still can see

My old home, mom and dad

All gathered 'round

...My Christmas Tree

Christmas Joy

A scowl, a smirk

Clearly they speak

Not ever saying one word

Eyes like daggers

A heart of stone

No friends, not one preferred

A life alone

Until one day

At church...the very last pew

You wandered in

For rest and warmth

And hear... Luke chapter 2

Sharp... the words

Piercing your heart

Inside... beginning to melt

Your heart of stone

Cracks and breaks

These feelings... you've never felt

Unto you is born

This day a Savior

Inside you know it's all true

Bowing your head

You call on Him

Now you know... He came for you

Changed completely

You stand to leave

Your mind on that baby boy

Scowls all gone

A thankful heart

Overflowing with…

Christmas Joy

Christmas Star

Light invading darkness

Like a beacon from afar

Rising slowly in the east

A new and glorious star

Beams of yellow and white

Across the Milky Way

Sent from God, a sign

Messiah is born this day

On a celestial highway

Prepared so long ago

Three men followed closely

To where...they didn't know

The star above stood still

They marveled at the sight

The newborn King awaits

In Bethlehem this night

A thousand slivers of light

Bright white with shades of blue

Shines 'round the holy scene

A...Glorious rendezvous

In a small and lowly home

Asleep...the newborn King

Unseen angels gathered 'round

Unheard songs as one they sing

Two thousand years ago

That first Christmas night

A star...a sign...a Savior

The Way, The Word, The

Light

Merry Christmas!

His Name

Closing my eyes in sleep
Drifting back in time
Searching thru the ages
A worthy name to find

A child has been born
The prophets long foretold
A Son; He has been given
Unspeakable gift behold

First begotten of God
Bright and Morning Star
The Alpha and Omega
Searched for wide and far

The Holy One of Israel
The Prince of Peace is He
King of all the ages
Salvations captain free

The Savior; The Messiah
He's Heir of all things
The First and the Last
I Am…King of Kings

Immanuel; Lamb of God
The Mighty One; The Word
Cornerstone and Counselor
Salvations Author heard

The Amen; Bread of Life
Jehovah; Redeemer; Friend
Nazarene... Solid Rock
Word of Life is penned

Reading the Holy Scriptures
Most worthy name I see
Great Son of the Highest
Jesus His name shalt be

His Name is
Jesus

Christmas

Morning

My journey complete

I rode into town

And quickly went to the Inn

Arriving to find

Only one room

With the census about to begin

My mind drifted back

To the couple I passed

So young, stopping to rest

I was sure going by

They were in need

Struggling, tired...distressed

Back downstairs

I saw them again

I could see she was with child

No rooms...out of time

About to give birth

Then a woman stopped...and smiled

My heart rejoiced

My guilt removed

As they slowly went down the street

There was a place

I could hear her say

A stable, nearby and discrete

That night at the Inn

My guilt returned

Unable to find any sleep

Thinking of them

Spending the night

That stable...with cattle and sheep

Restless my soul

Heavy my heart

Then a noise; very close by

Peace for my soul

First Christmas morn

At a newborn baby's first cry

Lights

After Thanksgiving

All over the town

Lights of the season

Turned on at sundown

Red, Green and blue

Orange and white

Steady and blinking

All through the night

Wrapped 'round chimneys

Hung on roof eves

Covering the bushes

Strung thru the trees

Necklaces blinking

Ear rings that flash

Wreaths on the car

Still blink when you crash

Lights burning brightly

Except for one place

Still dark in your heart

His Light...not a trace

This Christmas season

May darkness depart

May truth and Light

Shine bright in your heart

First Christmas morn

Jesus...The Light

No longer to walk

In darkness of night

Light of the world

Bright burning stays

Lighting our heart

Christmas Day...and always

Eyes So Blue

All through the town
Slowly lights fade
Snow on treetops
Shimmering jade

Still silent night
Walking Main Street
My home for these
My cold homeless feet

Living alone
This Holy Day
A long ten years
I've lived this way

At 2 am
The church bells ring
My frozen tears
Old memories bring

Lost in my mind
Then suddenly
A man…he stands
Right next to me

His hat pulled low
His coat drawn tight
He sat with me
This Christmas Eve night

My mind it raced
I wondered who
He slow looked up
With his eyes so blue

Such calming peace
All my fear erased
His gloveless hand
In my hand placed

He spoke no words
Just eyes of blue
His nail pierced hand
In mine...I knew

My melting heart
My frozen tears
Freed and thawed
Those bitter years

His heart, His hand
His love, I heard
With eyes so blue
...He
Spoke not a word

I'll not forget
That man, that night
That Christmas Eve
The colors bright

Your hand, Your touch

Those moments few

Your love for me

...and

Those eyes so blue

A Christmas Scene

Snow covered roof tops

Tree branches pure white

The moon and the stars

All light up the night

Distant bells ringing

Burnt wood in the air

Cold chill in the breeze

My mind, not a care

Peace in my valley

There's calm in my heart

No cards I need send

No shopping to start

Stare out my window

Take in all I see

Nature and Christmas

God's gifted to me

Kings on Bended Knee

A time and place

A perfect plan

One night, a rising star

Beautiful, bright

Like none before

Darkness illumined afar

Slowly moving

Across the sky

Followed on land by three

Mary...Joseph

A little child

Three Kings on bended knee

Winter Heart

I felt it today...
A change in the air
Slowly it's come once again

Like my past years
That have come...and gone
Change fools me now...and then

Change in my life and
A change in the breeze
The cold of winter is here

As my life goes by
A change in my heart
Like winters of yesteryear

The snow is falling
As I search my mind
Searching for tenderness lost

Just a young boy
Like a spring flower
Damaged by winters last frost

This winter unwelcome
Unwanted...so soon
Fall ending before it could start

The bitterness...the cold

Arriving to join...

The endless winter in my heart

My hope and prayer

And always will be

This year that winter will bring

The Joy of Christmas

A new spirit of love to

Change my winter heart to Spring

First Night

A shepherd boy...alone

This still and silent night

Sheep and shaded shadows

The moon and stars my light

A sudden burst of brilliance

The midnight sky was gone

Another world before me

Like a veil had been withdrawn

A voice so clear and strong

From where I could not tell

Fear not; I bring good tidings

Great joy…this first Noel

Unto you is born this day

A Savior, Christ the Lord

A child, He has been given

A King...to be adored

Ten thousand angels sang

I can't describe the sound

Nor the scene in Bethlehem

The stable...and child I found

A light so soft and pure

On Jesus where He lay

I knelt before Messiah

I had no words to say

I wondered; who am I

This sight that I should see

God's Son wrapped in glory

God's light His blanket be

That night in my heart stayed

Then I met Him once again

I shared with Him my story

Felt His peace as I did then

I told Him you're The One

The scriptures taught me true

Just a baby that first night

Yet I gave my heart to You

My life now nearly over

I'll soon with angels sing

My story with them I'll tell

That first night I

Met the King

Voices Fill the Sky

A story unconceived

Not scribed by quill or pen

A night like none other

Nor ever will again

The angels hand in hand

Compass the evening sky

Singing songs of praise

Sweet voices from on high

All mystery and wonder

That night the Savior came

A world filled with gladness

At...The whisper of His name

If I could journey back

In time... to anything

A shepherd boy I'd be

At the birth of my King

To see that silent night

To hear the baby's cry

Ten thousand angels singing

As...Sweet voices fill the sky

I Said Goodbye

A bridge...a box

My all night walks

No place to call my own

This road...I chose

Cold winter snows

Now reap what I have sown

Last night...I heard

A song, a word

A distant pleasant sound

Inside...I went
Old tattered tent
The joy of Christmas found

The folks...so kind
They didn't mind
My ragged unkept state

They welcomed me
They didn't see
A life that others hate

A song...The Word
I sang...I heard
I bowed my head to cry

I turned to leave

That Christmas Eve

My old life, I said

...goodbye

The Gift

Flawless...His plan

Eternal, pure and true

Perfect... His gift

A perfect gift for you

Never out of style

Timeless; just right

Personal... His gift

Personal for tonight

Gift of endless love

Forgiving even you

Unspeakable His gift

Sent tonight…brand new

Gift upon the table

Waiting for you there

Ask and you'll receive

Gift beyond compare

When this life is over

The gift; God will see

Hidden in your heart

Or ignored carelessly

The gift like any other

Gifts you must receive

Jesus waits for you

Unwrap Him and believe

Embers of My Dreams

Distant dreams, long ago

So many then...now few

Full of life, colors bright

Yellow, greens and blue

I dream I'll wake to find

God's gifts of peace and love

Wrapped by pure white angels

From His white throne above

Gazing at the evening sky

Lost in bright yellow beams

Moonlight brings to my mind

Embers of forgotten dreams

Warmth and joy fill my heart

Transcending time and space

My eyes now filled with glory

Angels sing; all fears erase

Snowflakes falling Christmas Eve

Bright white with shades of blue

A stable near, a baby's cry

Embers of my dreams come true

The Christmas Gift

Gifts all bright and pretty

Reflects the seasons spirit

All around the Christmas tree

So many; you can't get near it

The frenzy begins at seven

On that lively Christmas morn

The room in under a minute

Colored sea of paper torn

Soon the excitement fades

Wrong colors and sizes found

Toys broken or missing pieces

CD; won't make a sound

But isn't that always the way

On the surface things look great

After peeling away the layers

What's inside's not what they state

There was a perfect gift given

On the very first Christmas morn

So perfect; it's called unspeakable

First Christmas when Jesus was born

This Christmas up in the Smokies

The gift giving we've all forlorn

No packages are under the tree

Just ornaments…string popcorn

What about that first Christmas

And that very first Christmas gift

No pretty packages there to give

No piles to sort through and sift

A life sacrificially given

Promised with no blemish or flaw

Unwrapped that first Christmas morn

The promise; was just what we saw

A lesson there for our Christmas

Let's each be a gift to each other

Unwrapped nothing broken or missing

No need to exchange for another

A life that's committed to others

Not in word but lived out that way

This Smoky Mountain cabin Christmas

May it remind us of that first

Christmas Day

Note: This was written in the early morning while reflecting on a Christmas week spent up in the Smoky Mountains of Tennessee with family. We were about to leave the cabin for the long ride home and this was on my mind.

God Walked In

Hope for deliverance

Four hundred years

Silence from Heaven

Bitter the tears

A Remnant remained

Faithful and true

Brutally treated

Still waiting for You

Remembering words

Of Prophets of old

The promised Messiah

His coming foretold

Clinging to hope

Keeping His ways

Enduring the Romans

Cruelest of days

Until one night

In old Bethlehem

Virgin gave birth

And God walked in

Snowflake

Intricately formed

By His spoken Word

Billions have fallen

Not one ever heard

Each one unique

Beauty defined

Glorious they're made

One of a kind

Silently falling

From clouds on high

Floating on air

Like a butterfly

Like sparkling diamonds

In sunlight falling

Brilliantly reflecting

Their Heavenly calling

Blown to and fro

By the stormy gale

They'll perfectly land

Though delicately frail

One upon another

A shimmering cascade

A momentary display

So quickly to fade

A portrait of this life

Is each snowflakes tale

So delicate and short

Beautiful but frail

Our life is a vapor

Momentary then gone

Fades like the snowflake

As last breath is drawn

Soul and the snowflake

Both perfectly planned

Magnificently formed

By the Masters own hand

Christmas'

Missed

The snow is gently falling

On this holiest of nights

Alone, and no one calling

Just gazing at the lights

Thinking back to days gone by

Tonight, sorrow persists

Memories in good supply

Of all the Christmas' missed

There was a time years ago

When you were a younger man

A busy life was status quo

Unaware of His master plan

Friends, parties and the store

Were always on your mind

All those things came before

Needs to which you were blind

Later in life the blinders came away

From the eyes of your spirit and soul

The wages of your sins He did pay

By His grace you were made whole

Now your life has a purpose

Of peace and joy it consists

Though you're now an older man

There'll be no more Christmas' missed

Christmas Time

Scenes of seasons

Change with years

Replaying my life in my mind

I wonder tonight

If you're the same

Or in this, am I one of a kind?

When I was a boy

So selfish was I

Christmas was all about me

As years went by

My heart changed

Not once, but I see three

Christmas was gifts

When a young boy

Each year I just wanted more

My thinking changed

Stage two began

When I managed my CVS store

Gifts all forgotten

Christmas was sales

Focused on the shopping season

Hiring more people

Ordering more product

Each year missing the real reason

The years pass by

More changes in life

My Christmas time stage changed too

Gifts and the store

Have faded away

Now Christmas is all about You

Birth of the Savior

God amongst men

Greatest gift we've ever known

This Christmas time

And forever will be

About Jesus; about Him alone

Papa's Christmas

Sleigh bells ring, carolers sing

There's laughter in the air

Cookies, cake... all night awake

Excitement...everywhere

My Papa told of Christmas' old

I still remember well

T' was nineteen ten, a boy back then

His tales with me he'd tell

Horse and sleigh, the frozen bay
Beneath the amber moon

Lanterns dim, the tree we trim
Each season gone too soon

Christmas eve, we read, believe
That first Christmas day

Stories shared, my heart prepared
Papa's Christmas, still this way

Never the Same

I'm taking a look

Back through time

Back two thousand years

So much has changed

From then till now

Success and bitter tears

The mind of man

A gift from God

To think, create and dream

Has changed this world

For good...for bad

But change has been our theme

Once...only once

In all of time

Did a birth touch everyone

One starry night

In Bethlehem

When God gave us His Son

He changed the world

Touched every heart

Jesus would be His name

When He was born

Each soul...the world

Would be...never the same

About the Author:

Mitchell S Smith

Born and raised in New England, I now live in the Panhandle of Northwest Florida and have for the past ten years. I am currently working as a Region Manager for the Kroger Corporation.

I have always had a love and desire for reading and writing but have just started putting pen to paper, so to speak, in the past three years, as time has permitted. I never dreamed that I would be writing any poetry until three years ago, seemingly out of nowhere, on Christmas Eve day, it started. Feeling a little blue and reminiscing in my mind, the thoughts and feelings made their way to a word document in the form of a poem called "Christmas' Missed"...the release of feelings, sorrow and remorse that day when the poem was complete was wonderful and thus the poetry writing began. Three years later I have written just north of three hundred poems and it has changed me more than I could ever explain.

This fourth poetry book of twenty four poems, "A Christmas Journey...through poetry" has been a blessing to me and I hope and pray it will be to you as well.

Mitch

Other books by

Mitchell S Smith...

- Poems from the Heart; Romans 8:28
- Through Your Eyes
- Before...and After

Available on Amazon.com and other major on line book stores.

CPSIA information can be obtained
at www.ICGtesting.com
Printed in the USA
BVHW051435171022
649633BV00003B/145